TRACK & FIELD

GUIDE TO THE EVENTS

by Dan Zadra

Published by
The Children's Book Company
Mankato, Minnesota

Text/Design/Photography
by James Rothaus & Associates

Editor: Dan Zadra, Editor-In-Chief, YOUNG ATHLETE Magazine.
Bob Honey and Linda Carey, Design and Production.
Tom Horton, Photography.

The publisher wishes to acknowledge the
assistance of Men's Head Track Coach Charles A.
Petersen and Men's Head Cross-Country Coach
Mark Schuck of Mankato State University in the
preparation of this book.

Published by The Children's Book Company, P.O. Box 113,
Mankato, Minnesota 56001

ISBN: 0-89813-012-3

Library of Congress Number: 81-67698

In these pages you will find simple explanations of the different track and field events. You will also find explanations of the common terms used in track and field.

Use this book like your own track and field guide.

The fastest runners at a track meet are the sprinters. Like swift cheetahs on the African plains, sprinters are built for great speed over short distances.

The sprints are the shortest events in track. They cover 100 meters, 200 meters and 400 meters. Sprinters run at top speed from start to finish.

In the sprints the secret to a great time is a fast start. That's why sprinters practice coming out of the starting blocks over and over.

The 100-meter dash is one of the most exciting track events. At the sound of the starting gun, the sprinters burst out of the starting blocks and speed down the track, their legs and arms pumping furiously.

The holder of the world record for the 100-meter dash is often called the world's fastest human. The record for the 100-meter dash is just under 10 seconds.

In the 200-meter dash, runners sprint halfway around the track. A great time for the 200 is one under 20 seconds.

The longest sprint is the 400-dash. In this race, the sprinters run one complete lap of a metric–measured track. A world-class time in the 400 is one under 47 seconds.

5

If you decide to run in the distance events, you will need to work on endurance more than speed.

The distance races are as short as 800 meters (about one-half mile) and as long as the monstrous marathon (26 miles, 385 yards).

There are five distance races in track and field. They are: the 800-meter run, the 1,500-meter run, the 3,000-meter run, 5,000

meters, 10,000 meters and the marathon. High school meets might also include the so-called "metric mile" (1,600 meters) and "metric two-mile" (3,200 meters) instead of the 1,500–meter and 3,000–meter races.

The shortest distance events are the 800 and metric mile. Two laps around the track make up the 800 while it takes four laps to cover 1,500 meters. A good time in the 800 is under 1:50. In the 1,500 meters, Britain's Steve Ovett set a world record of 3:31.6 in August 1980. A year later, another British runner, Sebastian Coe, set a world record for the mile run at 3:47.33.

The 5,000-meter and the 10,000-meter races are events that tap the strength of even the best conditioned runners.

The final sprint to the finish line in a distance race is called a kick. This usually occurs in the last 100 meters of the race.

The marathon is the longest and most difficult event in all of track and field. The race covers 26 miles, 385 yards. Even a top marathoner runs for over two hours before hitting the finish line. Bill Rodgers, Frank Shorter, Henry Rono and Grete Waitz are among the world's best long distance runners.

THE HURDLES

There are four events that test a person's running and jumping ability. These are the hurdles.

Men run the 110-meter hurdles and the 400-meter intermediate hurdles. The intermediate distance in high school is 300 meters. The intermediate hurdles are 36 inches high. Hurdles for the 110-meter race are 42 inches (39 inches in high school). Women run the 100-meter and the 400-meter low hurdles (100-meter and 200-meter in high school). These hurdles are 30 inches high.

The secret to being a good hurdler is timing. Runners must time their jumps so they clear the hurdles without touching them or knocking them over. Even though there is no penalty for knocking down a hurdle, it often slows down a runner or makes him fall.

Renaldo Nehemiah was the first to break 13 seconds in setting a world-record time of 12.93 seconds in the 110-meter hurdles in August 1981. Fast times for the intermediate hurdles are under 50 seconds (men), 40 seconds (high school boys) and 60 seconds (women).

Edwin Moses and Debbie LaPlante are two of the other top hurdlers in the world today.

Teamwork is the key to having a winning relay team. Four runners must work together to complete the race.

THE RELAYS

In all relays a baton is the object that must be moved from the starting line to the finish line in the fastest way possible. Each runner carries a baton as he runs. When a relay runner is at the end of this part of the race, he will hand the baton to his teammate. This teammate then runs his part of the race and passes the baton to the next runner's hand.

There are many different kinds of relays, but the most popular are the 4 x 100-meter dash and the metric mile relay. Some high schools run the 800-meter and the 3,200-meter relays, too.

In the 4 x 100-meters dash, each runner sprints 100 meters before passing the baton to the next runner. In the mile relay, each runner sprints 400 meters before handing off.

The United states has always had world-record relay teams. That's why you see the names of Americans like Jesse Owens, Tommie Smith, Lee Evans, Wyomia Tyus, Evelyn Ashford and others in the record books.

LONG JUMP AND TRIPLE JUMP

Two of the field events, the long jump and the triple jump, take place at the jumping pit. The jumping pit is a 100-to-140-foot runway with a large sandbox at the end. The sand is used to cushion the jumpers when they land.

In the long jump, an athlete sprints down the runway at top speed. When he gets to the takeoff board, he jumps with all his might. The higher his body flies when he jumps, the farther he will travel. The distance of the jump is measured from the takeoff board to the jumper's first mark in the sand. If the jumper falls backwards, his jump will not be as long.

Bob Beamon, Larry Myricks, Ralph Boston and Jodi Anderson are some of the world's greatest jumpers. A great jump for men is over 25 feet; for women it is over 20 feet. The world record is an incredible leap of 29 feet.

Another jumping event, the triple event, is one of the oldest Olympic events. The triple jump is also called the hop, step and jump. Like a long jumper, the triple jumper sprints down the runway. But when he hits the takeoff board, he hops, then skips and finally jumps as far as he can. Only men compete in the triple jump. A very good jump is over 50 feet.

14

High jumpers may be the greatest leapers on earth. Imagine a man running 40 to 60 feet, then hurling himself over a bar seven feet high. Not only does it take great leaping ability to be a high jumper, but it also takes great strength and technique.

There are three techniques used by high jumpers. The first technique is one used by beginners. It is called the "scissors." Two advanced techniques are the "roll" and the "flop." Many people use the roll today, but the most popular technique is the flop.

Little Franklin Jacobs, who stands only 5-foot-8, has used the flop to high jump 7 feet, 7¼ inches — nearly two feet over his head.

Generally, tall athletes with long legs make the best high jumpers. But jumpers must also have good speed and concentration to be tops in their sport.

Dwight Stones, Dick Fosbury, Joni Huntley and Louise Ritter are top high jumpers in track and field history. Any jump over seven feet is good for men. For women, any jump over six feet is considered excellent.

HIGH JUMP

POLE VAULT

Some pole vaulters can soar over 18 feet in the air. That's why this event is the most dramatic and dangerous of all the track events. One slip and a pole vaulter might fall and be seriously injured.

The object of the pole vault is to use a pole to catapult over a very high bar.

In the old days, pole vaulters used stiff poles to jump. Today, they use a flexible fiberglass pole that almost throws them over the bar. Once the vaulter clears the bar, he falls to a bed of soft foam rubber.

Strong shoulders, arms and hands are needed to be a good pole vaulter. Speed is also important. But, above all, a pole vaulter must have courage.

Bob Seagren, Mike Tully and Earl Bell are some of the top pole vaulters in track history. A good vault is over 17 feet, but the 19-foot barrier was broken in 1981.

Shot Put: The object of the shot put is to throw an iron ball as far as possible. The men's shot put weighs 16 pounds (12 in high school); the women's weighs 13 pounds (just under 8 pounds, 2 ounces in high school). Size and strength are very important for this event, but quickness is the secret to being a good shot putter. Shot putters throw from a seven-foot circle that they cannot leave during the

throw. A good shot put for men is over 65 feet; for women anything over 58 feet is very good.

Discus: The object in the discus is to throw a flying saucer-like object as far as possible. The men's discus weighs 4 pounds, 6½ ounces (3 pounds, 9 ounces in high school); the women's, 2 pounds, 3$\frac{1}{8}$ ounces. The discus circle is eight feet, six inches across. Mac Wilkins, Al Oerter and Lorna Griffin have all been top U.S. discus throwers. For men, a throw over 220 feet is excellent; for women any throw over 200 feet is very good.

Javelin: In ancient times, men hunted with spears. Today, men no longer hunt with spears, but they do throw the javelin. The javelin is a long aluminum spear that is hurled into the air for distance. Bob Roggy, Duncan Atwood and Kate Schmidt have been top U.S. javelin throwers. Any throw over 275 feet (men) and 200 feet (women) is very good.

Hammer: The hammer looks like a shot put attached to a four-foot wire and handle. The total weight of the hammer is 16 pounds. The thrower tosses the weight after spinning around in a circle two times. Only large, strong men compete in the hammer. The best hammer throwers can send the weight over 230 feet out into the infield.

ANCHOR: The last runner of a relay team.

APPROACH: The run just before a throw or jump.

BATON: A hollow wand passed from one member of a relay team to another.

CARBOHYDRATES: The foods that provide most of our energy during exercise. Foods such as potatoes, bread, spaghetti, macaroni or bananas are good sources of carbo-hydrates.

CIRCLE: Where an athlete stands to throw the discus, shot or hammer. The athlete must stay in the circle for the entire throw.

CROSSBAR: A bar made of wood, plastic or metal. High jumpers and pole vaulters try to jump over the crossbar.

DEAD HEAT: A tie between two or more runners.

DECATHLON: A 10-event competition that lasts for two days. On the first day athletes compete against each other in the 100-meter dash, long jump, shot put, high jump and 400-meter dash. On the second day, they compete in the 100-meter hurdles, discus throw, pole vault, javelin throw, and 1,500-

A DICTIONARY OF TRACK AND FIELD TERMS

meter run. All the points are added up.

DISCUS: A field event in which the athlete throws a disc-shaped discus for distance.

EASY DAYS: Track stars are careful to schedule "easy days" of practice after hard days. Hard days are practices where you put almost full effort into your workout. Easy days should be spaced evenly between hard days. Easy days give tired muscles the chance to rebuild.

ENDURANCE: The ability to compete for long distances or long periods of time. Endurance can only be increased by training.

EXCHANGE ZONE: In relay races, the baton must be passed from one runner to another in

The discus looks like a flying saucer.

the exchange zone. This zone is usually 20 meters long.

FALSE START: When a runner leaves the starting block before the gun is fired. After a false start, all the runners must return to their starting block for another start.

FLATS: Track shoes that do not have spikes.

FLOP: One way of doing the high jump. In the flop, the athlete jumps headfirst over the bar with his back to the ground.

FLYAWAY: In pole vaulting, an athlete might choose to leave his pole at the very top of his vault. This is called a flyaway.

FOUL LINE: The line an athlete must stay behind in order to keep his jump or throw legal.

GUN LAP: The last lap of the race.

HANDOFF: When one runner passes the baton to another runner in a relay race.

HEAD WIND: A wind blowing against the front of a runner's body.

HEAT: A contest held before the final competition. An athlete must do well in a heat to qualify for the finals.

HURDLE: A barrier made of wood or metal

which runners must leap over in a hurdle race.

INSIDE LANE: The inside part of the running track. The lane closest to the infield.

JOG: To run slowly.

KICK: To speed up the pace near the end of a race.

LAP: One time around the track.

LEAD-OFF RUNNER: A relay team's first runner.

LONG DISTANCE: A term sometimes used for the 5,000-meter and 10,000-meter runs.

MARATHON: A foot race over roads or streets for 26 miles, 385 yards.

The shot is a heavy metal ball about the size of a grapefruit.

MEDLEY: A relay race in which the team members run different distances.

MIDDLE DISTANCE: A term that is sometimes given to the 800-meter and 1,500-meter runs.

OLYMPIC GAMES: The biggest, most important competition for the world's amateur athletes. The Olympics are held once every four years in a different country each time. Amateur athletes from dozens of countries around the world compete in friendship for gold, silver and bronze medals. The Winter Olympics and Summer Olympics are held a few months apart in the same Olympic year.

PACE: The rate of speed chosen by a runner.

PEAK: When an athlete paces his training so he will perform his very best on the day of an important competition.

PENTATHLON: A five-event contest for women. The events are the long jump, high jump, 200-meter dash, discus throw and 1,500-meter run. All the points are added up.

PIT: A soft landing area for a jumper.

PUT: When an athlete pushes the shot put in the air, his pushing motion is called a put.

RECEIVER: The runner in a relay race who is receiving the baton.

SALT TABLETS: Large tablets of salt which some runners take in hot weather. Salt tablets are supposed to replace the salt lost in sweating. But most doctors say that taking salt tablets is unnecessary and can be harmful.

SHOT: A metal ball made of iron or brass used in the shot-put competition. The shot can weigh between 8.13 and 16 pounds. It's about five inches in diameter.

SPRINT: A short, fast footrace up to 400 meters. Also called a DASH. Good sprinters have a high knee kick. They run straight ahead with no sideways movements of the legs or arms. A fast start is half the race.

STARTING BLOCKS: Runners place their feet against starting blocks to get a faster start. The starting blocks are anchored firmly to the track.

STEEPLECHASE: A race in which runners must jump over hurdles and a water jump.

STRADDLE: One way of clearing the high jump bar. In the straddle, the athlete clears the bar headfirst with his stomach facing the ground.

STRIDE: A step in running.

TRIAL: An attempt made in a field event.

TURN: The part of the track that is curved.

WESTERN ROLL: One way of clearing the high jump. In the western roll, the athlete clears the bar with his body turned sideways.

WINDED: An athlete is "winded" when he is so out of breath that he can barely breathe.

WINDSPRINT: A short, fast sprint.

Starting blocks help the sprinter get a faster start.

HOW TO UNDERSTAND TRACK MEASUREMENTS

Here in America we still measure most things in inches, feet, yards and miles.

Most of the rest of the world, however, uses the "metric system" of centimeters, meters and kilometers.

All official track and field events are now supposed to be measured in meters. The mile run sometimes is included in some meets.

There's no need to be confused if you are unfamiliar with metric measurements.

Just remember that one yard plus 3.37 inches is equal to one meter. And one mile is equal to 1.6093 kilometers.

On the next page are reference tables.

TRACK EVENTS

YARDS		METERS
40	equals	36.58
50	equals	45.72
60	equals	54.86
70	equals	64.01
75	equals	68.58
100	equals	91.44
110	equals	100.58
120	equals	109.73
220	equals	201.17
300	equals	274.32
440	equals	402.34
600	equals	548.64
880	equals	804.67
1,000	equals	914.40
1,340	equals	1,207.01

FIELD EVENTS

FEET		METERS
1	equals	.305
2	equals	.610
3	equals	.914
4	equals	1.219
5	equals	1.524
6	equals	1.829
7	equals	2.134
8	equals	2.438
9	equals	2.743
10	equals	3.048
20	equals	6.096
30	equals	9.144
40	equals	12.192
50	equals	15.240
60	equals	18.288
70	equals	21.336
80	equals	24.384
90	equals	27.432
100	equals	30.480
200	equals	60.960

TRACK EVENTS

METERS	MILES	YARDS	FEET	INCHES
1 equals 0		1	0	3.37
2 equals 0		2	0	6.74
3 equals 0		3	0	10.11
4 equals 0		4	1	1.48
5 equals 0		5	1	4.85
10 equals 0		10	2	9.70
20 equals 0		21	2	7.40
30 equals 0		32	2	5.10
40 equals 0		43	2	2.80
50 equals 0		54	2	.50
60 equals 0		65	1	10.20
70 equals 0		76	1	7.90
80 equals 0		87	1	5.60
90 equals 0		98	1	3.30
100 equals 0		109	1	1.00
110 equals 0		120	0	10.70
200 equals 0		218	2	2.00
300 equals 0		328	0	3.00
400 equals 0		437	1	4.00
500 equals 0		546	2	5.00
1,000 equals 0		1,093	1	10.00
1,500 equals 0		1,640	1	3.00
2,000 equals 1		427	0	8.00
2,500 equals 1		974	0	1.00
3,000 equals 1		1,520	2	6.00
5,000 equals 3		188	0	2.00
10,000 equals 6		376	0	4.00

TRACK EVENTS

MILES		KILOMETERS
1	equals	1.6093
2	equals	3.2187
3	equals	4.8280
4	equals	6.4374
5	equals	8.0467
6	equals	9.6561
7	equals	11.2654
8	equals	12.8748
9	equals	14.4841
10	equals	16.0935

TRACK
& FIELD

THE
CHILDREN'S
BOOK
COMPANY

FOR
YOUNG
PEOPLE